Alan Titchmarsh's · Gardening Guides

HERBS

HAMLYN

London · New York · Sydney · Toronto

Herbs in history

For flavouring soup, for weaving a magic spell or for killing off a deadly enemy, herbs have always been useful to man, and although the term 'herb' can be applied to any plant that dies down to the ground in winter, to most folk a herb is a plant that's used in the kitchen.

Herbs today might be thought of as a luxury, but before the discovery of modern drugs they were the living medicine chest attached to every house. There were herbs to sooth fevers, herbs to keep you regular, herbs to cure rashes, and a few to send the goblins scurrying away in terror.

Not all cures worked with great efficiency, but some of them did, and homoeopathy continues to thrive, using countless preparations based on herbs.

When smells in the city became as much of a problem as disease, the fragrance of herbs came into its own. Nosegays held close to the face presented a more pleasing perfume than open drains, and the arrangement of herbs in formal patterns within the garden, enabled them to be grown for ornament as well as health.

But it is in flavouring food that today's gardener finds herbs most useful. The Romans enjoyed spiced-up fare, too, and introduced many herbs to Britain. Many were lost during the Dark Ages, but returned during the Norman Conquests and have been with us ever since, livening up dishes that would otherwise be bland and boring. So be adventurous – don't stick to parsley and mint; try something new the next time you cook a Sunday lunch!

A 16th century woodcut of a raised herb bed

Herbs in the garden

There's absolutely no reason why you shouldn't spread your herbs all over the garden, but it does mean that you've got to remember just where each one is when you want a snippet for an omelette or a sprig for a salad. It's more convenient, and more fun, too, if you can grow them all in one place where their perfume will fill the air on warm summer days.

Nearly all herbs relish brilliant sunshine. Many of them come from warm countries and need sun to bring out their flavour as well as their aroma. Planted around a patio they'll enjoy life to the full, and you'll have the double pleasure of finding them easy to pick and pleasant to sit near.

Stepping stones make herb gathering more convenient

Bear in mind the height and spread of each herb (as well as it's form and colour) before deciding on its planting position. Some herbs are rampant and will swamp more delicate treasures. Plants like mint and lemon balm are rampageous. Plant them in bottomless buckets which can be sunk into the ground with their rims protruding. With any luck you'll be able to prevent their questing roots from exploring too far.

Spring is the best time to plant, though the fact that herbs can be bought in pots means that planting is possible at any time of year, provided that the soil's not dust dry or frozen solid.

Any reasonable soil will suit them. Don't go overboard on the manure; most herbs don't need it and will grow best in soil that's been dug or forked over and given just a sprinkling of fertiliser such as blood, bone and fishmeal. Too rich a soil will make herbs sappy and gross. In soil that's really poor and sandy, garden compost, peat or leafmould is helpful in holding moisture and bulking up the soil. Work it in a few weeks before planting.

Herbs for shade

If you simply don't possess a sunny spot there are just a few herbs that will grow in shade. Try these:

- Angelica
- Chervil
- Chives
- Lovage
- Mint
- Parsley

Curly-leaved parsley

Finding herbs

Most local nurseries and garden centres nowadays sell a good range of herbs in pots, but the best selection is offered by specialist nurseries. Buy in person if you can; it's more fun to choose the plants you want rather than to rely on them being chosen and sent through the post. Mind you, most mail order nurseries have a high standard of quality and you'll seldom be disappointed with the results, provided you give the plants a good start.

Water the plants an hour or two before they are to be planted. Remove their pots at planting time and, after digging a hole for the roots with a trowel, lower the plant in and firm back the earth really well. Don't plant too deeply – the 'crown' of the plant (where shoots meet roots) should be just below the surface of the soil. Herbs hate being buried too deeply, but they won't enjoy life if half their roots are above ground level.

Water the plants in thoroughly and don't let them dry out during their first year, otherwise they'll not establish a hefty root system that will lead to healthy growth in the future.

I've shown the height and spread of each herb in the A–Z section on page 14 to give you some idea of how far apart to set the plants.

Herbs in pots

Most herbs will grow a treat in pots, provided they can sink their roots into some reasonable compost and are well supplied with water and light.

They will never do well indoors. Herbs are hardy plants and simply grow tall and spindly in the heat and comparative gloom of a living room. Have a potful of basil by the sink if you want, but don't expect it to thrive for long.

If the pots can be stood on an outside windowsill the herbs will be fine. Here they'll receive plenty of light and fresh air which will result in good growth. They love to grow on balconies and roof gardens, too, so long as gales don't blow them away.

Young herb plants can generally be put into larger pots as soon as they are bought in spring. Plastic or clay pots 13cm (5in) in diameter are suitable, and will usually fit comfortably on an outside windowsill. Use John Innes No.2 potting compost, or a mixture of this and a peat-based compost such as Levington or Arthur Bowers. Peat-based compost alone tends to shrink when dry and herbs in pots are very quick to dry out.

Use the same compost mixture when herbs are being grown in window boxes, but whatever the container, make sure that it has plenty of drainage holes to allow excess water to escape. Badly drained containers will turn into muddy ponds in winter and herbs are notoriously bad swimmers.

As they grow the plants can be given larger pots. Spring is the best time for repotting. Use the same compost mixture as before and choose a pot that is 5cm (2in) larger in diameter. Old and tired herbs can be discarded in favour of young and healthy ones which can be bought or raised from seeds and cuttings (see page 12).

Patterns with herbs

The fact that they were once used in formal gardens and grown in intricate patterns has led herbs to be planted in

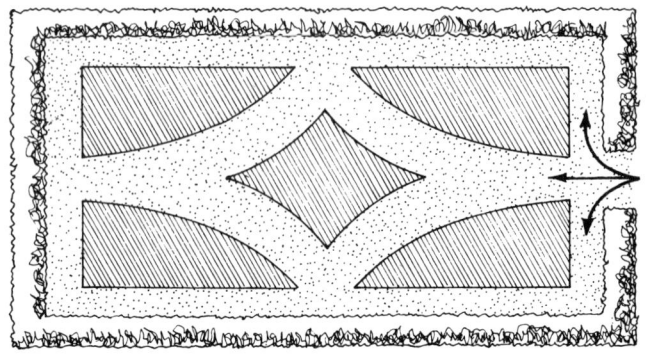

A simple design for a formal herb garden

all sorts of odd ways; some of which are mentioned below.

Old cartwheels can be painted and laid flat on the ground over prepared soil, and a different herb planted in each space between the spokes. If a long, narrow bed will fit more neatly into your plot than a circular one, use an old ladder instead of a cartwheel.

But it's more fun, and much more original, to make a formal garden to your own design using paving slabs or bricks and patches of herbs. There are countless patterns to be stitched with herbs and stonework to make a fragrant patchwork tapestry. All you need to do is bear in mind the relative heights and colours of your neighbouring herbs.

Harvesting and storing

Most herbs reach their peak of flavour just before they flower, and if they have to be stored for winter use, that's

A traditional knot garden planted with herbs

the time to gather them. Snip off suitable stems early in the day (taking them from all over the plant to leave it looking shapely) and dry them as quickly as possible. I know it looks pretty to have bunches of herbs hanging in the kitchen, but most of the flavour will be lost. Herbs need to be dried in a dark place, and the best bet is really a cool oven or an airing cupboard.

As soon as the leaves are crisp, strip them from the stems and crush them. To seal in flavour they should be stored in airtight containers that do not admit light. If they have to go in transparent jars, keep the jars in a dark cupboard. They'll store for at least a year. Herbs that dry well include:

- Rosemary
- Basil
- Sage
- Fennel
- Lemon Balm
- Bay

Lemon balm

Rosemary

Some herbs lose their flavour when dried and are better frozen. Wash the sprigs, dry them by patting with kitchen roll, then place them in polythene bags and put them straight in the freezer. They'll lose their shape when thawed but not much of their flavour. These are all recommended for freezing:

- Marjoram
- Parsley
- Chervil
- Tarragon
- Mint
- Lovage
- Chives
- Dill
- Fennel
- Basil

Chives   Lovage

Making more herbs

I will mention how each herb can be propagated in the A–Z Of Culinary Herbs, but it's worth giving just a few brief details of each method.

Seeds are easy to sow – simply fork over the patch of soil where they are to grow, lightly rake it level, scatter the seeds thinly over the surface and lightly rake again. Never let the soil dry out before the plants are well established. If the seedlings are crowded together, thin them out to leave one every 10cm (4in) or so. Wider spacings will be necessary for larger plants.

Division of large clumps can be carried out in spring or autumn, as a rule. Dig up the clump and pull it apart into fist-sized pieces which can be replanted at suitable spacings. Dead sections can be thrown away and any spares given to friends.

Cuttings of shoot tips are taken in summer and usually root quickest in a pot of seed and cuttings compost on a windowsill.

Cuttings of most herbs should be about 8cm (3in) long and sliced cleanly below a leaf joint at the base. Remove all the lower leaves before inserting the cuttings around the edge of the pot.

Extra humidity is always appreciated at this time and a polythene bag can be placed over the pot. Don't let the cuttings burn up in full sun.

Herb care

Don't forget that herbs are garden plants that need kindness, just like the brilliant bloomers in your summer bedding. Occasional feeds with liquid fertiliser will be beneficial in summer (two or three times between April and September will do them nicely).

Left to their own devices, many herbs become straggly. Clip them over with a pair of shears in spring if they make dense bushes, or pinch out the growing shoot tips if the stems are more sparse. Herbaceous herbs that die down in winter should have all their dead stems removed.

The golden form of lemon balm – see page 25

A–Z of culinary herbs

Angelica *(Angelica archangelica)*

One of the stateliest and most statuesque herbs you'll ever grow. The sturdy hollow flower stalk pushes up in the second year of the plant's life to a height of around 2.5m (8ft) and opens its white flowers on umbrella spokes in summer. The leaves are bold yet ferny, and a refreshing shade of green. Give the plant room to grow; it will spread 1 to 1.25m (3 to 4ft) across. As it is a biennial it should be sown afresh each year, to flower at the age of two.

Angelica is one of those rare herbs that prefers to grow in semi-shade. Sow the seeds in April or September in the soil where the plants are to grow.

Cut the flower stems for crystallizing in May or June, before the flowers are properly developed. Fresh leaves

Angelica

can be added to preserves, fruit compotes and cold drinks. Pieces of crystallized stem are used as decoration for cakes. The leaves can also be used to make tea, though it hardly ranks with Earl Gray when it comes to flavour.

Basil *(Ocimum basilicum)*

Basil is an annual, so however well you grow it you'll have to raise new plants from seed each spring. Scatter a few seeds in a pot of seed compost, cover them lightly with more compost and germinate them on the kitchen windowsill or in a warm, dark cupboard. When the seedlings are large enough to be handled they can be pricked out at the rate of one to an 8-cm (3-in) pot. Plant them in a sunny spot in the garden or in a pot stood outside in late May when danger of frost is past. Pinching out the shoot tips occasionally will help to keep them bushy. The leaves are glossy and green (or rich purple in

Basil

A statuesque angelica plant dominates this herb border

the variety 'Dark Opal') and the flowers small and white.

Basil will grow about 45cm (1½ft) high and wide, and fresh leaves can be gathered as soon as the plant is large enough. In late summer more leaves can be harvested and dried for winter use. Leaves also retain their flavour when frozen – those that are dried gradually become less flavoursome.

On buttered carrots and sliced tomatoes basil is a knock-out! It's also recommended for salads, soups and sauces, all kinds of meat, poultry and game, fish, cheese and pasta.

Bay *(Laurus nobilis)*

A bay bush in the garden will save you pounds over the years. It's an evergreen shrub and can be allowed to grow unrestricted or else clipped into lollipop or pyramidal shapes during summer. It's not as hard as nails, so find it a sunny and sheltered spot in well-drained soil. Better still,

Bay

grow it in a tub that can be taken into a frost-free greenhouse in winter. If tub-grown plants have to stay outdoors in winter, wrap sacking or straw around the container to offer a little insulation to the roots.

Plant bay trees in spring. Cuttings are difficult to root, so young plants are the best bet. Leave a bay tree to grow and it will reach 15m (50ft) and more, but it's easy to restrict by summer pruning – use the clippings in the kitchen.

Searing winter winds will cause leaf browning. Pick the fresh leaves at any time of year. Dry them in summer for winter use by friends. One leaf will flavour an entire meal.

Borage

Chervil

Borage *(Borago officinalis)*

Borage must be the easiest herb to grow. Scatter the seeds over a patch of sunny, well-drained soil in spring or autumn and plants will emerge every year thereafter. The leaves and stems are densely hairy and the nodding flowers are blue stars that shine all summer. Each plant will grow 60cm (2ft) high and as much across.

The flowers make a pretty garnish to fruit cups like Pimms, and the young leaves can be chopped and added to cheese or yoghurt, or else fried in pancake batter.

Caraway *(Carum carvi)*

It's the seeds of caraway that are used for flavouring. Sow them in late summer on a patch of sunny, well-drained soil where the plant is to grow and they'll be produced again at the end of the following year. Caraway is grown as a biennial and sown afresh each September.

The leaves look like finely cut parsley and the flowers like cow parsley, on a plant that is 60cm (2ft) high and 30cm (1ft) across.

Cut the stems just before the seeds are ripe and hang them up in paper bags so that all the seeds are caught. They are the traditional ingredient of seed cakes, and can also be added to cheese, cabbage, goulash and bread.

Chervil *(Anthriscus cerefolium)*

Chervil looks even more like cow parsley than caraway and grows to around 45cm ($1\frac{1}{2}$ft) high and 30cm (1ft) wide. Grow the plant as an annual, sowing the seeds on the soil where they are to grow in spring, and thinning out the seedlings while they are quite small. Dappled shade and a moisture-retentive soil are enjoyed.

The flavour is one of mild aniseed and the fresh leaves can be used during summer. Chop off the flowerheads. Chervil dries badly but can be frozen. It's a classic ingredient of 'fines herbes' and can be used to flavour all manner of dishes such as salads, game, omelettes, soups and sauces, eggs, cream cheese, fish and meat. It's a good garnish, too.

Chives *(Allium schoenoprasum)*

The daintiest of the onions, chives makes upright tufts of bright green leaves that are decorated with lilac-pink pom-pon flowers in summer. Cut the blooms off if you want the plant to retain all its flavour. It will grow about 23cm (9in) high and spreads to make a tidy clump in sun or dappled shade. Divide clumps in spring or autumn to make more plants or keep existing ones in check.

Chives enjoys any decent soil and benefits from having its faded foliage chopped off in spring. The leaves can be used fresh from early to late summer, and frozen for winter use. Their mild onion flavour perks up boiled eggs, cream cheese, soups and salads, fish, meat and poultry.

Coriander *(Coriandrum sativum)*

Often used but seldom grown, coriander is another of those herbs belonging to the parsley family, so its leaves are finely cut and its white or pale lilac flowers carried on umbrella-like heads. It's an annual, grows 45cm (1½ft) high and 30cm (1ft) across, and should be sown outdoors where it is to grow in spring. Well-drained soil and sun are essential. The fresh leaves can be cut in summer and used in curries and pickles, but it's the seeds that are most prized.

The plant will smell thoroughly unpleasant until the seeds ripen, then its full aroma is released. Gather the stalks and put them in bags to catch the ripening seeds. Use them to flavour ratatouille, soups and sauces, fish, meat, poultry, duck and game.

Dill *(Anethum graveolens)*

Like a miniature fennel at first glance, dill makes a feathery plant up to 60cm (2ft) or so high and has clusters of yellow flowers at the stem tips. It's an annual and needs to be sown afresh where it is to grow each spring, and though it enjoys a well-drained soil and sun, it isn't very happy in drought.

Fresh leaves can be cut and used as soon as the plants are large enough to rob; seeds are collected from the flowerheads just before they are shed naturally. Tie bunches of flower stalks in paper bags to catch your bounty. The leaves can be frozen, too.

Seeds are used in dill vinegar, pickles, bread and biscuits. Fresh leaves can be used in salads, cooked vegetables and egg dishes, as well as casseroles.

Dill

21

Fennel

Fennel *(Foeniculum vulgare)*

This graceful, feathery monster is a back-of-the-border plant in most gardens, but if you bring it forward within touching distance you'll be able to enjoy at close quarters the aniseed-scented filigree foliage. It grows a good 1.5m (5ft) high, and is best in its purple-leaved form, on which the acid-yellow flowers contrast well. It needs sun and well-drained soil and is perennial – once you've planted it it will stick around. Established clumps can be divided in spring; new plants can be raised from seed sown outdoors in spring.

Leaves can be used fresh in summer or frozen or dried. Stems are used in Provençale dishes. Leaves are good with sauces and soups, salads and stuffings, and with fish, lamb and pork.

Garlic *(Allium sativum)*

Garlic is a herb for gamblers (it needs a good summer) but it costs very little to buy a bulb in spring, split it into cloves and plant these 10cm (4in) apart as for onion sets.

The soil should be well cultivated and sharply drained, and by autumn plump bulbs should be ready for harvesting. Lift the bulbs and store them in a cool, dry, well-lit place once the leaves have started to turn yellow.

Use garlic in anything you like!

Horseradish *(Cochlearia armoracia)*

Plant this once and you'll never lose it. Large, green, dock-like leaves push up through the soil for quite a long way around, and will eventually give rise to 1.25-m (4-ft) stalks of white flowers in summer. It's really best restricted in a sunken enclosure of slates or tiles. It enjoys sun and a rich, moist soil. Pieces of the thick root can be planted in spring, and these form the best means of propagation.

It's the thick tap root that's used to make horseradish sauce, and it can be harvested at any time of year.

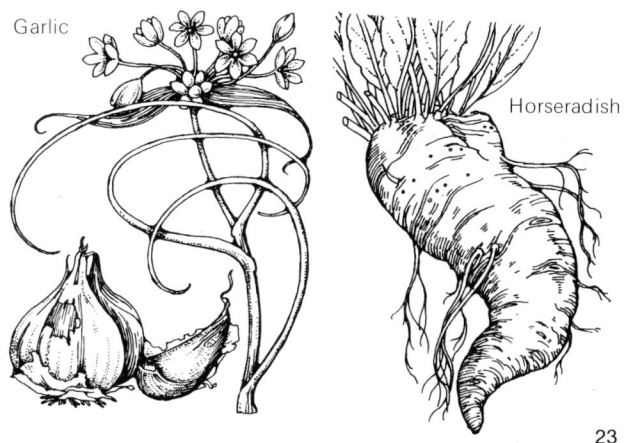

Garlic

Horseradish

Herbs in flower display a subtle range of colours

Lemon balm *(Melissa officinalis)*

Don't be fooled by that deceptively gentle name; balm is as rampant as mint. Grow it in a sunken bucket or similar enclosure to prevent it from swamping other plants. It's a perennial that will grow 60cm (2ft) high and even wider, and it is best in its golden form 'Aurea' and just as flavoursome. Its rough, oval leaves smell deliciously of lemons when crushed. The flowers are insignificant.

Plant balm in autumn or spring in any reasonable soil in sun or light shade. It is definitely perennial and divides easily in spring or autumn. Use fresh leaves in summer; dry or freeze them for winter. Good with fish, poultry, meat and salads. Crystallize the leaves for desserts.

Lovage *(Ligusticum officinale)*

Leaves like celery and umbrella-like flowers of pale green on towering stems give lovage a unique appearance. It grows to a stunning 2.5m (8ft) high, and 1.25m (4ft) across so needs plenty of room to stretch itself. Seeds sown in spring will produce flowering plants in the second year, and these will survive for a number of seasons. Rich soil in dappled shade is most enjoyed by this plant.

Mature plants can be divided in spring and the divisions replanted. Mind you, you'll not want many of these! Gather the leaves for use during the growing season. They freeze and dry well, too, retaining their zingy celery flavour. Use them in soups and stews and on salads. The seeds can be used for decorating bread and biscuits.

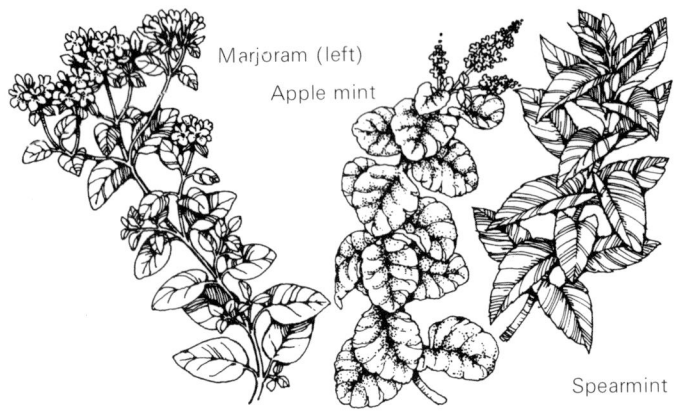

Marjoram (left)

Apple mint

Spearmint

Marjoram *(Origanum onites)*

Pot marjoram is a popular and easily accommodated herb with an appetizing aroma. It grows to around 30cm (1ft) high and rather more across and produces neat flower clusters that are usually pink; sometimes white. The leaves are small and rather downy.

Give marjoram a spot in full sun and a well-drained soil. Seeds can be sown where the plant is required to grow in spring, or mature clumps can be divided, also in spring. It's a perennial.

Harvest the leaves just before the plant flowers for maximum flavour. They freeze well. It's a versatile herb that's used in stews, soups and sauces, and with all manner of meats and vegetables. Try it and see.

Mint *(Mentha* species)

There are dozens of mints, scented of anything from Eau de Cologne to pineapple (though you'll have to use your imagination with some of them). They are all invasive and need to be grown in a sunken bottomless bucket or tin bath to prevent them from roaming too far. Division is the easiest form of propagation and can be carried out in autumn or spring.

Give mint a rich soil if you can; it will put up with sun or dappled shade but it doesn't enjoy drought. The purple flower spikes carried on stems up to 75cm (2½ft) high are a grand sight in summer.

Use fresh leaves whenever they are around to pick. They dry or freeze well and make delicious sauce for lamb. Try them also in savoury butter, as a garnish in fruit cups or crystallized.

Parsley *(Petroselinum crispum)*

The frilly and crispy leaves of parsley hardly need to be described, but do remember that the herb is best sown afresh each year. Too many gardeners try to keep a clump going for ever. It's a neat plant, growing about 15cm (6in) high and it makes a good edging to flower beds and vegetable patches.

Sow the seeds where they are to grow in spring. Be patient; they take ages to germinate but an overnight soak in water before sowing will hurry them up. Find a spot in sun or dappled shade. The plant is a biennial and will gradually become delapidated in its second year. Gather fresh all the year round if you can protect a few plants with cloches; otherwise freeze some leaves for winter use. Add the leaves to whatever you like, especially parsley sauce, Maître d'Hôtel butter and bouquet garni. The leaves are the classic garnish used in pubs and restaurants.

Variegated- and purple-leaved cultivars of sage

Rosemary *(Rosmarinus officinalis)*

Although it suffers in really severe winters, rosemary will usually come through unscathed to continue pushing upwards its spire-like stems, thickly clothed in narrow, dark green leaves that are sweetly savoury. It is evergreen and a valuable backbone shrub in any sunny, well-drained border, and with any luck its pale lavender flowers will decorate the stems every spring. It usually grows to around 1.25m (4ft) and as much across, but in spots where it is happy it may be even taller.

Cuttings of firm shoot tips will root in a pot or outdoors from mid- to late summer. Leave them for a year before transplanting them.

Use fresh leaves all the year round in sauces and soups, with lamb, chicken and pork and in stuffings.

Sage *(Salvia officinalis)*

The coloured-leaved cultivars of sage such as 'Icterina', yellow and green; 'Tricolor', pink, purple and cream; and 'Purpurea', soft mauve, are just as good in the kitchen as the plain green form, and even more decorative in the garden. The leaves of all are attractively felted, and the plants make neat hummocks around 45cm (18in) high and even more across. Plant them in well-drained soil in a sunny spot, and propagate them from stem tip cuttings in summer – they will root easily in a pot of compost covered with a polythene bag and stood on a windowsill. Clip back the shoots of old and tatty plants in spring.

Harvest fresh nearly all the year round, but the offerings are meagre in winter so dry or freeze some summer leaves. A traditional ingredient of stuffings; good, too, in soups and sauces, with pork and poultry.

Sorrel *(Rumex acetosa)*

Vinegar leaves, we called them as kids. Rather like a miniature dock in appearance, with arrowhead leaves and spikes of green summer flowers, sorrel will grow to around 30cm (1ft) and maybe 15cm (6in) across. Any ordinary soil, and a spot in full sun or the lightest shade will keep it happy. It's a perennial and can be divided for propagation purposes in spring or autumn, or seeds can be sown where the plants are to grow in spring.

Use the leaves fresh as soon as the plant is large enough to withstand defoliation. Dry or freeze them in summer for winter use. Leaves can be cooked in soups and sauces, and used to flavour salads and vegetables.

Tarragon *(Artemisia dracunculus)*

It's the French tarragon, rather than the Russian, which has the best flavour. It's a perennial with narrow green leaves on stems around 60cm (2ft) high, and it needs a sunny, sheltered spot, preferably at the foot of a south- or west-facing wall. Cover it with straw or bracken when it dies down in winter. Make sure the soil is well drained. Divide mature clumps to make more plants in spring.

Harvest fresh in summer, and freeze a few leaves at the same time. Use to make tarragon vinegar, and to flavour salad dressings and mustard, butter and sauces, as well as with eggs, fish, meat and poultry. Fresh, chopped leaves can be used as a garnish on salads.

Thyme *(Thymus* species*)*

As with mint, there are various flavours of thyme, from the traditional savoury kind to the lemon-scented ones. All are small and spreading perennial shrubs with tiny, aromatic evergreen leaves. They'll make clumps up to 23cm (9in) or so high and three times as much across. They adore sun and any well-drained soil, and their flowers of pinkish mauve add greatly to their attraction. Clip over and divide mature clumps in spring, or sow seeds at the same time where the plants are to grow.

Use the leaves fresh all the year round, though their flavour is at its height just before flowering. Dry or freeze some stems for winter use. Vital in bouquet garni; in stuffings and sauces. Use with poultry, game, fish and meat, salads and cooked vegetables.

Winter savoury *(Satureja montana)*

A neat little shrub with narrow, dark, evergreen leaves. It grows 30cm (1ft) high and about 45cm (1½ft) across. Bright sunshine and a well-drained soil are essential. Sow the seeds where they are to grow in spring, or divide mature clumps at the same time. Protection with a cloche or straw will help the plant through the winter in the north and in exposed situations.

Harvest fresh sprigs all the year round. Use as for sage and on all manner of cooked vegetables.

Tarragon   Winter savoury

Index

Page numbers in italics refer to illustrations

angelica 5, 14, *14*, *16*

basil 10, 11, 15, *15*
bay 10, 17, *17*
bed, raised *3*
borage *18*, 19
buying 6

caraway 19
care 12–13
chervil 5, 11, *18*, 19
chives 5, 11, *11*, 20
coriander 20

dill 11, 21, *21*
drying 10

fennel 10, 11, 22, *22*
fertiliser 5, 12
freezing 11

garlic 22, *23*

harvesting 8–11
history 2
homoeopathy 2
horseradish 23, *23*

knot garden *9*

lemon balm 4, 10, *10*, *13*,
    25
lovage 5, 11, *11*, 25

manure 5
marjoram 11, 26, *26*
medicine 2
mint 4, 11, 26
  apple *26*
  spearmint *26*

parsley 5, 11, 27
patio 3
planting 4, 6–8
  in pots 6
  in shade 5
  indoors 6
propagation 12

rosemary 10, *10*, 29

sage 10, *28*, 29
savoury, winter 31, *31*
sorrel 30
storing 8–11

tarragon 11, 30, *31*
thyme 30

winter savoury 31, *31*